Children of the Bible

christian art kids

© 2017 Christian Art Kids,
an imprint of Christian Art Publishers,
PO Box 1599, Vereeniging, 1930, RSA

359 Longview Drive, Bloomingdale, IL, 60108, USA

First edition 2017

Cover designed by Christian Art Kids

Illustrations by Catherine Groenewald

Unless otherwise indicated, all Scripture quotations are taken from the *Holy Bible*,
New Living Translation®, copyright © 1996, 2004, 2007, 2013, 2015 by
Tyndale House Foundation. Used by permission of Tyndale House Publishers, Inc.,
Carol Stream, Illinois 60188. All rights reserved.

Scripture quotations marked CEV are taken from the *Holy Bible*,
Contemporary English Version®. Copyright © 1995 by American Bible Society.
All rights reserved.

Scripture quotations marked NCV are taken from the *Holy Bible*,
New Century Version®. Copyright © 2005 by Thomas Nelson.
Used by permission. All rights reserved.

Printed in China

ISBN 978-1-4321-1570-8

18 19 20 21 22 23 24 25 26 27 – 11 10 9 8 7 6 5 4 3 2

Contents

Introduction

God Loves Children Very Much!

God has a special place in His heart for children. He thinks so highly of them that He tells adults and parents to be more like children. It's true! You can read the story in Luke 18:15-17 (CEV):

Some people brought their little children for Jesus to bless. But when His disciples saw them doing this, they told the people to stop bothering Him. So Jesus called the children over to Him and said, "Let the children come to Me! Don't try to stop them. People who are like these children belong to God's kingdom. You will never get into God's kingdom unless you enter it like a child!"

The children of the Bible were ordinary kids just like you and your friends. Some were obedient and very brave. Others were scared and lonely. Some had their likes and dislikes and might not have liked to eat their vegetables either. But God had a special plan for each of His children in the Bible. The plans of some worked out nicely because they obeyed God. The plans of others didn't work out, because they were disobedient.

God also has a special plan for our lives. He created each of us in a special and unique way. Some of us are tall while others are short. Some are loud and others are quiet. Some of us are as busy as bees, while others like to take it easy. God even has a plan with the freckles on the tip of your nose and your curly hair!

He wants us to help Him to make His plan work! All we have to do is to love Him and try our best to obey Him.

God loves us very much. His love surrounds us like a warm and cozy invisible blanket that covers all His children. We don't have to be rich or pretty or clever. We don't have to wear fancy clothes for Him to notice us. Deep inside our hearts we all have a special label saying: **Made by God, with love.**

We are all perfect just the way we are.

God knows that we often make mistakes. He is glad when we say we're sorry and ask for another chance.

Let's find out what we can learn from the children of the Bible.

Cain and Abel, the First Brothers

Abel took care of flocks, and Cain became a farmer.
Genesis 4:2 NCV

Adam and Eve lived in the Garden of Eden. It must have felt like a long holiday. They had enough food and all the animals were their friends. God visited them every day. Then the three of them walked through the garden and talked about all kinds of things.

After Adam and Eve listened to the snake, everything changed. They had to leave the garden and work hard to find food to eat. The animals were also not so friendly anymore. Adam and Eve were no longer able to walk and chat to God like they had done before.

Even though Adam and Eve sinned, God still loved them. He didn't want them to suffer. So He gave them a special surprise – a baby boy. His name was Cain. Adam and Eve were overjoyed. God was also glad. He wants His children to be happy.

Shortly afterwards God gave them another boy. His name was Abel. "Now we are a family of four!" said Adam and Eve. They were so happy. The two brothers were very different from each other. Cain loved to work in the garden. He probably built dams and dug around in the ground. Sometimes he helped his dad, Adam, to sow seeds and plant flowers. By the time he got home he was always covered in mud. "I'm going to have my own garden one day, Mommy!" said Cain when Eve bathed him.

Abel loved animals. He often played with the pet lamb. Eve just laughed when he tried to hide the little lamb under his blanket at bedtime. Sometimes Abel walked with Adam to the sheepfold. "I am going to look after my own sheep one day, Dad!" said Abel.

The boys grew up quickly. It was not long before Cain was old enough to help Adam in the garden all day long. He was upset when the flowers died because it didn't rain. He became angry and stamped his feet. Adam and Eve worried about his temper.

Abel was also old enough to take the sheep out to the field on his own. The little lambs were playful and even sucked Abel's fingers. At sunset Abel went home humming a cheerful tune. The sheep followed him. Eve heard them coming from afar.

One day, many years later when the brothers were grown, they decided it was time to bring offerings to God. It was their way to thank Him for everything. Cain and Abel collected dry pieces of wood and neatly stacked them together. Cain put fruit and veggies on his pile. Abel offered meat. Then they set it on fire.

Abel's offering burned with big flames and lots of smoke. "Look, Cain!" he called out. "God likes my offering!" Cain's offering didn't even make a small flame. He sulked.

God saw everything. He said to Cain, "If you do things well, I will accept your offering. But be careful! Sin is ready to attack you like a wild animal. Sin constantly wants you, but you must rule over it." Cain didn't listen to a single word. He was busy making evil plans. "Let's go out into the field again," he told Abel.

While they were out in the field, Cain attacked his brother, Abel, and killed him. "Where is your brother?" God wanted to know from Cain. "I don't know. I'm not his caretaker!" Cain answered angrily. "I will have to punish you," God said. "You will plough the ground, but it will not grow good crops for you anymore, and you will wander around on the earth for the rest of your life."

Cain had a fright. "Don't punish me like that, please!" he pleaded with God. "Everyone will want to kill me." "I will look after you," said God. Then the Lord put a special mark on Cain's forehead. The mark would warn anyone who met him not to kill him.

Adam and Eve were very sad. Their dear Abel was dead and Cain had to go away. Now it was only the two of them.

Sometimes we are also like Cain and Abel. We fight and lie and are jealous of each other. But God wants us to do what is right. We must try to be patient, kind and forgiving with each other.

Isaac Learned That God Always Provides

"God will provide a sheep for the burnt offering, my son,"
Abraham answered. And they both walked on together.
Genesis 22:8

Isaac was a very special boy. Abraham and Sarah waited for many years before he was born. They waited so long that Abraham began to wonder if they would ever have a baby.

One night God led Abraham outside. "Look at the stars," God said. "One day you will have many grandchildren and great-grandchildren, more than all the stars in the sky. This whole country will belong to you and your family. All will be well. I will take care of you."

Abraham believed every word that God said. He knew that God always kept His promises. But sometimes it is just so hard to have to wait. Abraham was 100 years old when Isaac was finally born. "You see, it was all worth the wait. Our little boy, Isaac, is such an adorable little boy!"

Sarah tickled Isaac until he laughed. "He is so cute and so very clever!" said Sarah. She knew that since Isaac's birth, Abraham loved God even more. He would do anything for Him.

When Isaac was about 11 years old, God decided to test Abraham's faith. He said, "Take Isaac to the land of Moriah. Sacrifice him as a burnt offering on one of the mountains." Abraham decided to obey God, but his heart was breaking into a million pieces. Early the next day he woke Isaac up. "Let's go to the land of Moriah and make an offering there," he said. "Start packing our things. I will cut the wood for a fire for a burnt offering. The donkey can carry the wood." Then Abraham, Isaac and two servants left. Isaac chatted, laughed and made jokes all the way. Every now and then he picked up a round and shiny little stone and put it in his pocket. Abraham didn't say a word. He couldn't stop thinking about the terrible thing he had to do.

On the third day they reached the foot of the mountain. Abraham told the two servants, "Stay here with the donkey. My son and I will go over there and worship, and then we will come back to you."

Then Abraham took the wood for the sacrifice and gave it to Isaac to carry. He also took a big knife and the flint. Together they walked to the place God told Abraham.

"Daddy?" Isaac asked after a while.

"Yes, my son," answered Abraham.

"Dad, we have the wood and the flint, but where is the sheep for the burnt offering?" "Don't worry, Son," answered Abraham. "God will give us the sheep to offer."

Finally they reached the place that God had told Abraham about. While Isaac was collecting more stones,

Abraham offloaded the donkey. He built an altar and laid the wood on top. Abraham then picked up a big knife and got ready to kill his son as a sacrifice.

Suddenly an angel of the Lord called out from heaven: "Abraham, stop! Put away the knife and don't hurt your son!"

Abraham was so relieved. God knew that he was willing to sacrifice his only son. He passed the test of faith!

At that moment they heard something in the nearby bushes. It was a ram. His horns were stuck in the branches. Abraham took the ram and sacrificed it as a burnt offering in place of Isaac.

"From now on we will call this place 'The Lord Provides!'" said Abraham.

God was very pleased with Abraham. "You were willing to sacrifice your dear son, Isaac," He said. "I will surely bless you. The land will belong to you and your children. All will be well with you."

Back at home Isaac took out all the stones from his pocket and arranged them in a beautiful pattern. "What are you doing with all these stones?" Abraham asked. "It's for the Lord," said Isaac, "because He provides."

God did not let Isaac and his father down. He will also never let you down. When it seems like you have a problem and you can't find a way to fix it, God will surprise you with a great plan!

Ishmael, the Little Boy in the Desert

"Go to him and comfort him, for I will make
a great nation from his descendants."
Genesis 21:18

As we have just read, Isaac was Abraham and Sarah's only son. But Abraham had an older son too. His name was Ishmael and his mother's name was Hagar. Hagar worked for Isaac's mom, Sarah.

Ishmael was much bigger and stronger than Isaac. When Isaac was little, Ishmael carried him around on his back. Other times Ishmael showed Isaac how to use a slingshot and build little boats that floated on the water. This made their dad, Abraham, very happy.

But there was one problem. Ishmael's mom, Hagar, and Isaac's mom, Sarah, would sometimes argue. At such times the boys would also fight. One day there was a great feast. Everyone sang, ate and had a good time. The children were dressed in their best clothes, and enjoyed all the nice food. Suddenly Sarah saw how Ishmael made fun of her little boy, Isaac. She went to Abraham and said, "Enough is enough! It is time you get rid of Hagar and Ishmael. There is no place for a slave and her son in this house!"

Abraham was very sad. He loved his whole family very much. He didn't want to chase Ishmael and his mother away. God saw that Abraham was sad. "Don't be troubled about Ishmael and Hagar," God said. "Do whatever Sarah tells you. I will look after Ishmael and Hagar. You'll see, one day Ishmael will have many children and grandchildren."

Abraham listened to God. The next day he packed food for Hagar and Ishmael, and gave them some water in a leather bag. Then he said goodbye and sent them away. While Ishmael and Hagar went on their way, they often looked back at Abraham. They didn't really know where they were supposed to go. Abraham was very sad. He stood and watched until he couldn't see them anymore. *God will take care of them,* he thought. *He promised.*

After a day or two Ishmael and Hagar's food was finished. Another day later the water was also finished. "I'm hungry, Mommy!" cried Ishmael. Hagar opened the cloth in which she carried their bread. There were just a few crumbs left. She scraped them together and gave it to Ishmael.

"I'm thirsty, Mommy," cried Ishmael shortly afterwards. Hagar emptied the last drops of water into her hand. She wet Ishmael's dry lips with the last bit of water and hugged him tightly.

After a while she picked him up and continued walking. But the sun was very hot and she was getting weaker. Finally she put her son down in the shade under a bush. She sat down a little further and cried. *I don't want to watch my son die of thirst,* she thought.

Suddenly Hagar heard a voice. It was an angel!

"What is wrong, Hagar?" asked the angel. "You don't have to be sad. Your son won't die. God has heard your boy crying. Pick him up and comfort him. He will have many children one day." Just as the angel finished speaking Hagar saw a well of water. The water was clear and cool. Hagar couldn't believe her eyes. She grabbed the leather water bag and filled it with water. Ishmael drank and drank until the water ran down his chin. Then it was his mother's turn. She also washed Ishmael's face and hands. Then she sat down with her tired feet in the cool water.

"God helped us to find water," she told Ishmael. "He will also help us find a way out of the desert."

And that was exactly what happened. From that day on God was with Ishmael. He grew up to be a strong and very courageous man. He loved the desert and enjoyed hunting. He had many children and grandchildren. He became the father of a great nation ... just as God had promised!

Always remember that God keeps His promises. He makes a way for us even when there seems to be no way out of a problem.

Jacob and Esau, the Disobedient Twins

As the boys grew up, Esau became a skillful hunter. He was an outdoorsman, but Jacob had a quiet temperament, preferring to stay at home.
Genesis 25:27

Abraham and Sarah were very proud of Isaac. Especially when he married the beautiful Rebekah and they expected twins. But the two babies were as busy as little bees. They pushed each other in their mother's belly. It made Rebekah very tired.

"What must I do, Lord?" she asked.

"Two nations are fighting in your belly," answered the Lord. "The one will be stronger than the other. The older brother will always do what the younger one says."

Isaac and Rebekah were very happy when their boys were born. They called the first boy Esau. His skin had a reddish color, and his body was covered in fine hair. The second boy was named Jacob. He had a fair skin.

As a small boy Esau loved nature. Rebekah had to watch him closely, otherwise his short little legs waddled off into the fields. When she was not looking, he chewed on bugs and played with ants. It wasn't long before he pretended to hunt wolves and bears. Jacob was the shy one. He didn't like to leave the house. He helped his mom in the kitchen.

A few years later the two boys were all grown up. Esau hunted bears and wolves. Jacob prepared delicious meals.

One day Esau returned from the field. He was tired and hungry. "Mmmm, something smells good! What is it?" he wanted to know. "It is lentil stew," answered Jacob.

"Can I have some? I am starving!" asked Esau.

Suddenly Jacob had a bright idea. "Not before you sell me your rights as the firstborn son," he said.

"You can have anything you want, just give me some of the stew!" said Esau.

Jacob gave Esau some of the stew. He also gave him some bread to eat with it. While Esau ate, Jacob thought, *That was a clever plan! When our father dies, I will inherit everything.*

Weeks passed by, and the weeks became months and years. Isaac was very old and almost blind. One day he called Esau, "Go hunt in the field for an animal for me to eat," he said. "Then bring the tasty food to me. I want to bless you before I die."

Rebekah heard what Isaac said. She ran to Jacob and said, "Go out to our goats and bring me two of the best young ones. I will prepare them just the way your father likes them. When you take the food to him, he will bless you instead of Esau."

"It won't work, Mom," said Jacob. "Esau is hairy and my skin is smooth."

"Just do as I say," answered Rebekah.

So Jacob went out and got the two goats. Rebekah prepared the food, just like Isaac liked it. She told Jacob to wear Esau's best clothes. Then she took the skins of the goats and put them around Jacob's hands and neck. "There you go," said Rebekah. "Now you can take the food to your father."

"Who are you?" Isaac asked.

"It is me, Esau," Jacob lied.

"How did you find the animal so quickly?" Isaac wanted to know.

"God helped me," Jacob lied again.

"Come closer so that I can touch you, then I will know if you are really Esau," said Isaac.

Jacob moved closer. "Your voice sounds like Jacob, but your hands are hairy like Esau's," said Isaac. "Are you really my firstborn son, Esau?"

"Yes, Dad, I am," Jacob lied.

"Give me my food so that I can eat and bless you," said Isaac. When Isaac finished eating, he blessed Jacob.

Not long afterwards Esau returned from his hunting trip. He was very upset! "It's the second time that Jacob has tricked me," he cried. "Don't you have a blessing left for me, Dad?"

"My poor child, there is nothing left to give you," Isaac said sadly.

"If I get my hands on that brother of mine, I am going to wring his neck!" shouted Esau. Rebekah heard everything. She ran to Jacob. "Go to your Uncle Laban. Stay there until it's safe for you to return."

Jacob didn't want to leave, but he had no choice. "I made a mess of things, I won't tell a single lie ever again!"

Jacob learned his lesson. He realized that telling a small lie is like a wave in the ocean. It gets bigger and bigger until it knocks you off your feet!

Joseph and His Coat of Many Colors

Jacob loved Joseph more than he did any of his other sons ... Jacob had given Joseph a fancy coat.
Genesis 37:3 CEV

After many years Jacob and Esau made peace. By that time, Jacob was one of the richest men in Canaan. He almost had more donkeys, sheep, goats and cattle than he could count. It wasn't important to him. He was just glad to see Esau again. And all the people were also happy for him. The women and children sang and danced all night long.

Then Jacob called one of his boys. His name was Joseph, and he was Jacob's favorite. "Say hello to your uncle," said Jacob. Joseph ran and greeted him. Just like his dad taught him. "You look just like your grandpa, Isaac," said Esau and gave him a pat on the back.

The time passed by quickly and soon Joseph was big like his other ten brothers. It was only, Benjamin, his younger brother, who was smaller than him.

He sometimes went with his brothers to take care of the sheep. But there was one tiny problem. Joseph was a tattle-tail. To make matters worse, he was Jacob's favorite son and he made Joseph a special coat. It was the most beautiful coat with long sleeves and colorful patterns. The patterns were all the colors of the rainbow. His brothers were jealous.

"Joseph thinks he's so clever!" one of his brothers complained. "Dad has never given any one of us such a beautiful coat," said another one. Joseph was so impressed with his coat that he didn't even realize his brothers were jealous and upset with him. He waved his arms so that the long sleeves of his coat swished around.

It wasn't just the coat that was causing problems. Joseph also had strange dreams. First he dreamed that they were all working in the field, tying up bundles of wheat. Suddenly Joseph's bundle stood up, and his brothers' bundles gathered around and bowed before his. Joseph couldn't wait to tell his brothers about his dream.

They didn't think it was funny. "Do you really think you're going to be king and rule over us?" they asked angrily.

The next night Joseph had another dream. This time the sun, moon and eleven stars bowed before him. Joseph actually told his brothers about this dream as well. They were even angrier than the first time. "If you think Mom, Dad and all of us are going to bow in front of you, you're making a big mistake!" they shouted.

One day Joseph's brothers took the sheep to graze far from their home. Jacob wondered how they were doing.

He sent Joseph to go and find out. His brothers saw Joseph coming. "There comes the dreamer!" hissed one brother. "Let's get rid of him!" said another one. "Yes!" shouted the rest. "Let's kill him and throw him into a pit. Then we will never have to listen to his silly stories again. We can tell Dad that wild animals ate him."

Reuben, the oldest brother, didn't like this plan. "Please don't murder or harm him. Let's just throw him in a well," he said. The other brothers didn't know that Reuben had a plan. He wanted to rescue Joseph and take him back to his father.

When Joseph reached his brothers, they pulled off his colorful coat and threw him into a dry well. While the brothers sat down to eat, merchants on camels came past on their way to Egypt.

One of Joseph's brothers, Judah, jumped up. "Let's sell him to these merchants," he said. "It's better than killing our own brother." The brothers looked at each other and all agreed.

So the brothers took Joseph out of the well and sold him to the merchants for eight ounces of silver. Reuben didn't know what was happening because he didn't eat with them. When he returned and found that Joseph was gone, he was very upset. He cried and begged, but it was too late. Only the footprints of the merchants and the camels and Joseph were left behind.

The brothers killed a goat and dipped Joseph's coat in the blood. Back at home they gave the coat to Jacob. He was devastated. He thought that Joseph had been eaten by a vicious animal. They tried to comfort him, but it didn't help.

"I will be sad about my loving son Joseph until I die!" he sobbed.

Meanwhile, Joseph arrived in Egypt. He was alone. He didn't have his brothers or his father or his beautiful coat with him. But God was with him. It was the beginning of a great adventure for him! God turned what seemed like a hopeless situation for Joseph into something great. Joseph ended up as second-in-command in Egypt and saved many people, including his family, from starvation.

Moses in the Basket

When she could no longer hide him, she got a basket
made of papyrus reeds and waterproofed it with tar
and pitch. She put the baby in the basket and laid it
among the reeds along the bank of the Nile River.
Exodus 2:3

Joseph, his dad, Jacob, and all his brothers lived in Egypt for the rest of their lives. They had more grandchildren and great-grandchildren than they could count. Finally there were so many of them that the Egyptians started calling them "Israelites." Everybody knew that the Israelites were God's people. They tried their best to obey Him. God cared for them like a father cares for his children.

Pharaoh, the king of Egypt, didn't like it. *The Israelites are too many and too strong for us to handle!* he thought. *One of these days we will no longer be in control of our own country.* Then he made a wicked plan. He commanded his soldiers, "Kill all the Israelite baby boys!" The poor mothers cried and begged, but it made no difference.

One mommy already had a little boy and a girl. Their names were Aaron and Miriam. When she had another baby boy, she decided to hide him. Then she made a basket of reeds and covered it with tar so that it would float and not sink. She put the baby in the basket and walked down to the river. There she put the basket in the river and let it float. "Dear God, I love this little boy so much," she prayed. "Please keep him safe!"

Miriam watched the basket from a distance. She picked flowers and collected feathers in the meantime. When her baby brother became restless, she sang to him.

One day the king's daughter came to the river to take a bath. Her servant girls came with her.

Suddenly the princess called out, "Look! A basket!" Shortly after the princess was standing with Moses in her arms. "This must be an Israelite baby," she said. "He is the cutest little boy. I want to take him home with me." "Whaa!" cried the little boy.

"Poor thing, he must be hungry," said the princess.

"Where will we find milk to feed him?" one of the servant girls asked. "Who will look after him?" another one wanted to know.

Miriam quietly came out of her hiding place. "I know an Israelite woman who can nurse him for you," she said very courageously. "That's an excellent idea!" said the princess very impressed.

Miriam ran like the wind and called her own mommy.

"Feed this little baby," instructed the princess. "And I will pay you for it." Miriam's mother couldn't believe it. God answered her prayers!

When the boy was big enough, his mother took him to the palace. They quickly walked past the vicious-looking guards. But none of them were allowed to hurt the boy. He was special. The princess adopted him as her own son. She said, "I will call you Moses, because I pulled you out of the water."

From that day Moses lived in the palace like a real prince.

The days became months and the months became years. Moses became a clever and obedient young man. There was just one problem. The Egyptians treated the Israelites very badly. And it bothered Moses a lot. One day he saw an Egyptian man hitting an Israelite. He became so angry when he saw it that he killed the Egyptian. *Oh no! What have I done?* He was scared and fled to Midian.

In Midian Moses' life was different than in the palace. He had to look after sheep. One day he took them up Mount Horeb which was God's mountain.

The sheep were uneasy. The birds didn't make a sound. Even the itty-bitty bugs hid under the rocks. Then Moses saw a burning bush. The flames crackled and there was smoke everywhere, but the bush didn't burn up. *This is strange,* thought Moses and walked closer.

Suddenly God spoke to him from the flames, "Moses! Moses!" The flames were so bright Moses had to cover his eyes. "Here I am, Lord," answered Moses. "Do not come any closer," said God. "Take off your shoes. You are standing on holy ground. I am the God who looked after Abraham, Isaac and Jacob. I've seen how badly the Egyptians are treating My people. I have come down to save them. I am going to lead them to a beautiful land with lots of food. And you have to show them the way!"

Moses was terrified. "How on earth will I manage to do that?" he wanted to know. "Don't worry," God answered. "I will be with you and help you."

Wow! God works in amazing ways! Who would have thought that Moses, who was chosen to lead the Israelites through the desert, was once a boy whom his mother had hid in a basket on the river?

41

Samson, the Boy with the Long Hair

"You will become pregnant and have a son. You must never cut his hair, because he will be a Nazirite, given to God from birth. He will begin to save Israel from the power of the Philistines."
Judges 13:5 NCV

The Israelites were without hope. For forty years the Philistines had been treating them very badly. They wished God would send someone to save them. Manoah and his wife also felt hopeless. They were unhappy because they couldn't have any children.

One day a messenger of God appeared to Manoah's wife. "You will soon become pregnant and have a baby boy," he said with a smile. "From now on don't drink wine or beer or eat unhealthy food. This little boy will belong to God from the day of his birth. He will save Israel from the power of the Philistines. You must raise him in a very special way and never cut his hair." Manoah's wife couldn't wait to tell the good news to her husband. "But we've never had any children," said Manoah concerned. "How will we know how to raise him in a special way? I will pray and ask God to send us the messenger again. He must explain to us exactly what to do."

"That is a great idea!" said Manoah's wife. "I can think of a million things to ask him!"

God was glad that Manoah and his wife wanted to do their best for Him. He sent a messenger to explain everything carefully to them.

"Please stay awhile so we can cook a meal for you," Manoah invited the messenger when he finished speaking.

"Rather offer a burnt offering to thank the Lord," said the messenger. So Manoah sacrificed a young goat and offered some grain as a gift to the Lord. While they were watching the flames, the messenger suddenly went up to heaven in the flames. Manoah and his wife had such a big fright they bowed face down to the ground. "The messenger was an angel from God!" said Manoah. "Yes, you are right!" said his wife. "God must love us very much, otherwise He would never have allowed such a wonderful thing to happen to us."

A while later the special boy was born. Manoah and his wife called him Samson. As he grew older his hair became longer and longer. God blessed him just as He promised.

It wasn't long before God's Spirit made Samson so strong that he killed a lion with his bare hands. When the Philistines made Samson angry, he grabbed the jawbone of a donkey and killed a thousand men with it. A while later they surrounded the place in the city where Samson was. He got so angry that he took hold of the doors and the two posts of the city gate. He carried them on his shoulders to the top of the hill. This made the Philistines think twice before bullying the Israelites again.

One day Samson saw Delilah. She was beautiful. Samson didn't even feel like fighting with the people anymore. He just wanted to look at Delilah the whole day long. The Philistines saw this. They told Delilah: "Find out what makes Samson so strong, and we will give you a lot of money."

Delilah nagged Samson day after day. She wanted to know the secret to his strength. One day Samson couldn't take it anymore. "If someone shaved my head, I would lose my strength and be as weak as any other man," he finally said. *Now I know the secret!* Delilah thought. She waited until Samson fell asleep and cut all his hair. Then she called the Philistines to capture Samson. They blinded him and put him in prison. Poor Samson had to work as a slave. He felt as if everyone had forgotten about him, but God hadn't. He still

loved Samson just as much as when he was a little boy. God's Spirit still burned like a tiny flame inside Samson's heart.

"Let's make fun of Samson!" the Philistines decided one day while they were celebrating at a feast. So they brought Samson from the prison to perform for them. They made him stand between the pillars. Nobody noticed that his hair had grown back. While the Philistines mocked Samson, he prayed to God, "Please give me strength once more."

Suddenly God's Spirit burned like a great fire inside Samson. He put his arms around the two pillars and shouted. Then he pulled with all his strength. By the time the Philistines realized what was going on, it was too late. The building had collapsed on them.

When Samson obeyed God he had incredible strength. But when he disobeyed, God took his strength away. Always remember to obey God and then you will be able to do great things for Him too.

God Calls Samuel

The Lᴏʀᴅ came and called as before, "Samuel! Samuel!"
And Samuel replied, "Speak, Your servant is listening."
1 Samuel 3:10

Hannah and her husband, Elkanah, were sad. They didn't have any children. One day they went to the temple in Shiloh. Hannah prayed softly, "Lord, I am Your servant. You see how sad I am. Please give me a baby boy. I promise to give him back to work for You."

Eli, the priest, didn't know Hannah was praying. He only saw her lips move. Eli thought she was drunk and he scolded her.

"No, Sir, you're making a mistake," said Hannah. "I'm just sad."

Eli felt bad that he was so rude to Hannah. "May God give you what you asked for," he said.

Soon after that God gave Hannah and Elkanah the cutest baby boy. Hannah was very happy! "His name is Samuel because I asked the Lord for him," she said.

When Samuel was old enough, Hannah and Elkanah took him to the temple. Eli was very impressed. Finally he had a helper. His own sons, Hophni and Phinehas, were two disobedient boys who didn't listen to their father and didn't care about God.

Eli loved God very much. He taught Samuel to love God just as much. And he taught him everything about the tabernacle and the Ark of the Covenant.

Hannah and Elkanah came to visit Samuel every year. They knew the Lord and all the people coming to the temple liked Samuel a lot. Hannah was so proud of Samuel that she gave him a coat that she made every time she visited him.

One night Samuel heard a voice calling him: "Samuel! Samuel!"

"Here I am!" he answered and ran to Eli. "You've probably dreamed. I didn't call you," said Eli.

Samuel went back to bed and was just under his blanket when he heard the voice calling him again: "Samuel! Samuel!"

"Here I am!" answered Samuel and ran to Eli again. But Eli said, "I didn't call you. Go back to bed." So Samuel went back to bed.

The Lord called Samuel for the third time. Samuel got up and went to Eli and said, "I am here. You called me."

Eli finally realized that it was the Lord who was speaking to Samuel and smiled. "I think it is the Lord who is calling you," he

said. "If He calls you again, say, 'Speak, Lord, Your servant is listening.'"

Samuel felt a little scared. He had never before heard the Lord speak to him. "Don't worry," comforted Eli, "just do as I've said." Samuel just got back in bed when the Lord called again: "Samuel! Samuel!"

This time Samuel knew what to do. "Speak, Lord, Your servant is listening," he answered very bravely.

And God spoke to Samuel. He told him all kinds of things. He also had a message for Eli. "I am going to punish him because he knows his sons refuse to respect Me and he let them get away with it!" warned God.

Samuel waited until the next morning. He got up and dressed himself. He wished he didn't have to give the message to Eli. He rather went to the temple and opened the doors.

Eli knew Samuel well. He saw the boy was worried. "Come here, my boy," he said. "Tell me everything that the Lord said to you. I promise I will not be angry with you."

Samuel told him everything. When he finished talking he was out of breath. Then Eli said, "He is the Lord. Let Him do what He thinks is best."

Samuel didn't exactly know what this all meant. All he knew was that the Lord spoke to him. And that was awesome!

From that day on God spoke to him often. Samuel became a great prophet. God gave him messages to tell to the Israelites. Everyone knew that they could count on Samuel.

Hophni and Phinehas Are Disobedient

The sons of Eli were scoundrels
who had no respect for the Lord.
1 Samuel 2:12

Samuel made Eli very happy. He was diligent and a good example to others. Eli wished his two sons, Hophni and Phinehas, could be more like Samuel. They were two really bad boys. They didn't have any respect for Eli or for the Lord. When it was their turn to work in the temple, they would send a servant to take the meat that was still boiling for the offerings and bring it to them. If the Israelites didn't want to give their offerings, Hophni and Phinehas bullied them.

Eli was old and tired, and his eyesight was failing. To make matters worse he heard more and more stories of his badly-behaved sons. One day Eli called the two boys. "Why are people telling all these terrible stories about you?" Eli wanted to know. "You must stop doing these things. If you sin against God, you will get punished!"

"Oh, please, Dad!" was all that Hophni and Phinehas said.

They didn't listen to Eli and continued causing trouble. Later Eli became so ashamed of them that he pretended not to see what they were doing. But the Lord saw everything. One day He sent a man to Eli with this message: "I have always been very proud of your family. Therefore, I have chosen you from all the families of Israel to work in the temple. Your sons are doing very bad things. You are their father, and you should have punished them a long time ago. Because you didn't, I have to punish you now. There will come a time when you and your family will not be so important anymore. Everyone in your family will die at a young age, and you will be very concerned about the temple. Your two sons, Hophni

and Phinehas, will die on the same day. I will appoint a faithful priest who will do what I ask. Each of your surviving family will bow before him and beg for food and money."

Eli's worries just got bigger and bigger. At least Samuel was a ray of sunshine in his life. He brought lots of cheerfulness and warmth into the old priest's life. Samuel didn't know that he was going to be the faithful priest whom God's messenger spoke about.

One day the Israelites were fighting against the Philistines. Before long 4,000 people were killed. "We will have to make a plan, and fast!" said one of the Israelite leaders. "Let's bring the Ark of the Covenant of the Lord from Shiloh and take it with us into battle. Then God will save us from our enemies." It was not long before the Ark of the Covenant arrived at the Israelites' camp. And guess who came with to look after it? None other than Eli's disobedient sons, Hophni and Phinehas.

The Israelites were so happy and cheered so loudly that the ground shook! "Oh dear, what is all the shouting about?" wondered the Philistines. When they were told it was because the Ark of the Lord had arrived, they panicked.

"It's the same God who destroyed the Egyptians with all those plagues!" they said to each other. "Today we must fight like never before. Otherwise we will become their slaves!"

The Philistines fought desperately and easily defeated the Israelites. They took the Ark of God and also killed Eli's two disobedient sons.

A messenger ran from the battle back to Shiloh as fast as he could. He found Eli alongside the road. Eli knew of nothing that had happened. He was 98 years old and completely blind. He was sitting on a chair near the town's entrance to hear the news of the battle.

He was very worried about the Ark and about his two sons. "What happened my child?" Eli wanted to know. "The Philistines defeated us," said the messenger. "Many of our people have been killed. Your two sons, Hophni and Phinehas, were also killed. The Philistines captured the Ark of the Covenant."

When Eli heard the bad news, he fell backward off his chair and died.

Samuel was very sad about his friend. He felt sad because Hophni and Phinehas refused to listen to their father. *Things could have been so different if they had just listened to Eli,* he thought.

But Samuel also realized that God knows best. He was satisfied to stay behind alone and give God's messages to the Israelites. That was what he wanted to do his whole life ... from that very first time that God called his name!

A Shepherd Boy Defeats a Giant

David replied to the Philistine, "You come to me with sword, spear, and javelin, but I come to you in the name of the LORD of Heaven's Armies – the God of the armies of Israel, whom you have defied. Today the LORD will conquer you, and I will kill you and cut off your head."
1 Samuel 17:45-46

One day the Israelites said to Samuel, "All the other nations have kings. Only we don't have one. Give us a king who wears a crown and lives in a palace. Someone who is very strong, brave and clever. He will help us defeat the Philistines."

God helped Samuel to find the right king. His name was Saul. He was a warrior. The Israelites were very impressed. "King Saul will help us defeat the Philistines!" they shouted.

Shortly afterwards King Saul's soldiers and the Philistines put up camp on either sides of a small stream. Among King Saul's army were three brothers. They also had a younger brother named David. He was still too young to fight in battle. He looked after his father's sheep and played the harp.

David was not big and strong, but God loved him very much. God saw the goodness inside David's heart.

One day a giant Philistine warrior was looking for trouble. His name was Goliath. He was three meters tall and wore special armor made of metal. His spear was thick and heavy. King Saul and his men were terrified of him.

"Don't you want to fight me, or are you too scared?" shouted the big bully beating on his chest.

In the distance someone was coming. It was David. His father had sent him to bring food to his brothers and cheese for their captain. He heard how Goliath made fun of the Israelites.

"Who is that Philistine who mocks God's children like that?" David wanted to know from the soldiers.

"I wish someone can teach him a lesson," one soldier sighed.

"The one who can do that will be allowed to marry the princess and will be very rich," said another one.

David went to King Saul and said, "Don't worry about the giant. I will fight against him."

"Don't be silly!" said King Saul. "You are only a boy, and he has been a soldier for a very long time."

"I've been looking after my father's sheep for many years, and I've slain lions and bears many times," said David. "God, who rescued me from them, will also rescue me from this Philistine!"

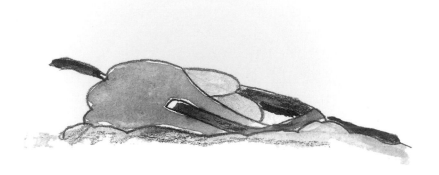

Saul could only shake his head. "All right, go ahead," he said. "May the Lord help you." Then Saul gave David his own armor and strapped his sword over it. Poor David could barely walk. So he took the armor off again.

Without thinking twice David took his shepherd's stick and sling in his hand and walked to the small stream. There he picked up five smooth stones and put them in his bag. Goliath saw David and came closer. "You are just a boy!" he shouted. "Come here so that I can destroy you!"

David wasn't bothered by the big giant. "You come to me with a sword, spear and javelin," he said. "I come to you in the name of the God of Israel. Today the Lord will conquer you. Then everyone will know who the God of Israel is!"

Suddenly Goliath moved closer to David to attack him. David didn't waste any time. He ran quickly to meet the giant, while reaching into his bag and taking out a stone. He hurled it with his sling and *swish!* the stone flew through the air and hit Goliath *bam!* against the forehead. The big bully stumbled and fell face down on the ground. Then David used Goliath's sword and cut off his head.

The Philistines were so scared. They ran away as fast as they could. "Hooray!" Hooray!" shouted the Israelites as the Philistines fled.

When David was asked by people, "Did you really manage to kill the giant with one single stone?" he replied, "No, I did it in the Name of God. That's the best weapon anyone can have!"

A Little Boy Gets His Mommy Back

King Solomon said, "Don't kill him. Give the baby to the first woman, because she is the real mother." When the people of Israel heard about King Solomon's decision, they respected him very much. They saw he had wisdom from God to make the right decisions.
1 Kings 3:27-28 NCV

Some time later, David became king. He did his best to please God. He looked after the Israelites and helped them to stand together. He also brought back the Ark of the Covenant from Jerusalem, and made plans to build a new temple. But God said, "You have done enough now. Your son, Solomon, can build the temple one day." King David listened. God always knows best.

Many years later Solomon became king. One night God spoke to Solomon in a dream. "What can I give you?" God asked. "Lord, I really want to be obedient to You and have an understanding heart," Solomon answered. "I want to be wise, so that I can always know the difference between right and wrong."

God was very proud of Solomon. "You make My heart glad!" He said. "You could have asked to live a long time or to be rich. Or you could have asked for your enemies to be destroyed. Instead, you asked for wisdom to make right decisions. So I'll make you wiser than anyone who has ever lived or ever will live. I will make you very rich and very wise, and you'll be greater than any other king. If you obey Me and follow My commands, as your father David did, I'll let you live a long time."

When Solomon woke up he was very grateful towards God. He immediately started to make burnt offerings to God, and he gave a feast for all his leaders and officers.

Soon everyone knew how clever and wise King Solomon was. People came from all over to ask for his advice. One day two women came to Solomon. "My master, this woman and I live in the same house," said the one woman. "My baby boy was born three days before her baby. One night while we were all asleep she rolled over on her baby and he died. Then she quietly took my son from my bed while I was asleep and put the dead baby in my bed. But she can't fool me. I knew immediately that it wasn't my little boy!"

"No, that's not true!" said the second woman. "The living baby is my son, and the dead baby is hers!"

"That's a lie!" said the first woman.

"No, it's not!"

"That's enough," said King Solomon calmly.

The two women were quiet. "Bring my sword," instructed the king. "Now cut the living baby into two pieces, and give each woman half."

The real mother of the living baby couldn't believe her ears. She fell down before the king and begged him, "Please, don't kill my little boy! Rather give the baby to her. But please don't hurt him!"

"That's okay. Cut the baby into two pieces!" said the second woman.

King Solomon smiled. "Stop right now! Give the baby boy to the first woman, because she is the real mother!"

The little boy's real mommy hugged him tight. She didn't know how to thank King Solomon.

Everyone heard about the story of the little boy who was given back to his real mother. "King Solomon is the best and wisest king in the entire world. God sent him to us!" said the Israelites.

And the little boy's mommy?

From that day on she told him the bedtime story of God's wise king who helped her get her precious baby back.

A Little Boy Comes Back to Life

Then he lay down on the child's body, placing his mouth
on the child's mouth, his eyes on the child's eyes, and
his hands on the child's hands. And as he stretched out
on him, the child's body began to grow warm again!
2 Kings 4:34

Close to the town of Shunem lived a farmer, his wife and their little boy. One morning the farmer was walking to his fields where his workers were busy harvesting. "Wait for me, Daddy!" called the little boy and ran after him.

The two were barely in the fields when the little boy started complaining that his head hurt. The farmer immediately sent him back home with a servant. The boy's mother held him on her lap, but he just became sicker and sicker. By the afternoon, the little boy died.

His mother picked him up and carried him to the room where the prophet Elisha always used to sleep when he visited them. Then she shut the door and said to her husband, "Send a servant and a donkey. I want to go to Elisha. I won't be gone for long."

"Why?" her husband wanted to know.

"Don't worry, everything will be fine," she said and left immediately.

Elisha saw her coming from a distance. He sent his servant, Gehazi, to greet her. But she was in such a hurry that she chased right past him. When she reached Elisha she fell down on the ground before him and grabbed his feet. Gehazi wanted to stop her, but Elisha said, "Leave her. She is very upset. I can see something is wrong."

"Oh Master," cried the woman, "you know the Lord gave me and my husband one child, a boy. And now he is dead."

"Gehazi!" said Elisha, "Get ready. Take my walking stick with you. Don't talk to anyone along the way. Just go straight to the little boy and lay my walking stick on his face."

"Master, you must come with us!" cried the woman. "All right," said Elisha and went with them.

In the meantime Gehazi went ahead and laid the walking stick on the boy's face, but nothing happened. Finally Elisha and the mother reached the house. Elisha went into the room where the boy was laying on the bed and locked the door behind him. Then he started to pray to the Lord.

He went to the bed and lay on the boy, putting his head on the boy's head, his eyes on the boy's eyes, and his hands on the little boy's hands. Slowly the boy's body became warm. All of a sudden the boy sneezed seven times, and then he opened his eyes and looked at Elisha. "I want my mommy," he said with a trembling voice.

"Gehazi!" called Elisha, "Go get the boy's mother!"

The two were back in no time. "Here is your child!" Elisha said with a big smile.

The woman bowed down before Elisha. She was so grateful that God had helped him to bring her only son back to life.

"I love you, Mommy!" said the little boy and put his chubby little arms around her neck. He knew nothing about what had happened to him. But one day, when he was old enough, he came to understand all about how special he and all the children of the world are to God.

A Servant Girl Saves the Commander's Life

One day the girl said to her mistress, "I wish
my master would go to see the prophet in Samaria.
He would heal him of his leprosy."
2 Kings 5:3

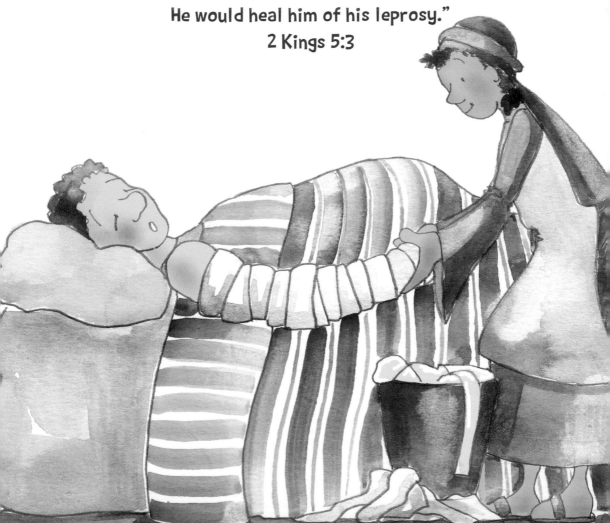

Naaman was a very important man. He was the commander of the Aramean army and a friend of the king. Naaman wore grand clothes and lived in a very big house with many servants. There was just one problem. He suffered from a terrible skin disease called leprosy.

When you are a leper, your hair falls out, your body is covered in sores and finally you die of this terrible illness. All the people with leprosy in Naaman's time were chased out of town. They had to stay alone so that they couldn't infect others.

Poor Naaman. Neither his money nor all the king's doctors could heal him. There used to be a lot of people in his fancy house, but since he became sick everyone stayed away. Not even the servants could stand to watch Naaman's sores.

There was one girl who didn't treat him differently. She was a servant girl from Israel who worked for Naaman's wife. The Lord was present in the girl's heart. He helped her not to feel sick when she looked at Naaman. She was still just as friendly and helpful as before.

One would never say that she was far away from her family and her hometown. Every time she smiled Naaman's heart felt a little lighter for a while. The girl knew that the people from her hometown couldn't stop talking about the great prophet Elisha. God gave him the strength to do miracles. He even made a child who was dead come back to life. She knew God would also help Elisha to heal her master.

So the little girl said to Naaman's wife, "I wish my master would go see the prophet Elisha in Samaria. He will heal him for sure!" Naaman's wife immediately told him. Naaman was so excited that he told the king about it. "What are you waiting for?" the king asked. "I will send a letter with you."

Not long after that Naaman left. He took precious gifts with him: gold, silver and ten sets of clothes. In his pocket was the letter from the king. It said: "I am sending my servant Naaman to you to heal him from his skin disease."

When Naaman finally reached Elisha's house, he sent a messenger out who told Naaman: "Go wash yourself in the Jordan River seven times. And your skin will be healed."

But Naaman was very angry. "Elisha didn't even come out of his house to greet me," he moaned. "And why should I wash myself in the Jordan River? Our rivers are better than all the waters of Israel!"

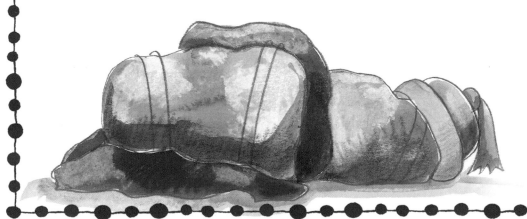

Naaman's servants tried to calm him down, "Commander, if Elisha told you to do something great, you would've done it, right?"

"Yes, I suppose so," Naaman mumbled.

"But now he gave you a simple task. Don't you think you must do what he said? Maybe it will work and you will be healed?"

And that is exactly what Naaman did. He went and dipped himself in the Jordan River seven times. The next moment all his terrible sores were gone. His skin became new and smooth like the skin of a child.

"No one will ever stare at my skin again. My house will be a happy and cheerful place again!" Naaman called out with joy.

He knew that the servant girl who worked for his wife had helped to save his life. He knew that her God and Elisha's God was the only true God. From that day he didn't want to serve any other gods.

He decided to go back to Elisha and gave him the gifts to thank him. Elisha just shook his head. "It was not me who healed you. It was the Lord," he said.

Naaman went home. He couldn't wait to tell the good news to the servant girl from Israel and thank God.

Little King Josiah Completes a Huge Task

Josiah was eight years old when he became king, and he reigned in Jerusalem thirty-one years. He did what was pleasing in the Lord's sight and followed the example of his ancestor David. He did not turn away from doing what was right.

2 Kings 22:1-2

Josiah's father was King Amon. Josiah knew his father and many other Israelites didn't serve God but worshiped all kinds of other gods. One day he overheard a small group of people, who still served God, talk. They were worried because his father didn't do anything to make God's heart glad.

One day, when Josiah was eight years old, a terrible thing happened. Josiah's father was murdered. The Israelites were very angry. They caught the killers and punished them severely. Then they called Josiah and said that he must be king in his father's place. The next moment they poured oil on his head and anointed him as the king. Everyone bowed before Josiah and called him "Your Majesty!"

All of a sudden the beautiful gardens of the palace were not his playground anymore. They became the place where he worked and had to attend important meetings. Fortunately, Josiah's mom and many advisers were always by his side to help him. They showed him what to do and how to do it. Josiah learned quickly. Every day he did his best to please God. Everyone was very proud of him. "Well done, you are a great king, just like King David!" they said.

They were right. Josiah's name didn't mean "the Lord supports" for nothing. God was busy preparing him for a big task. He had to help the Israelites turn back to the Lord.

A few years later Josiah said, "It's time to get rid of all the idols in Israel." They first destroyed all the altars. Then all the places where gods were worshiped were smashed to pieces and only dust was left behind. "Right," said Josiah, "now it's time to fix the temple of the Lord!"

The builders got to work immediately. The priest, Hilkiah, made sure everything went smoothly. One day he sent Josiah a very old book with God's laws written in it. But when Josiah read what was written in this book, he was so upset that he tore his clothes. "The Lord must be very angry with us because we don't live according to His laws," Josiah cried.

Josiah decided to send Hilkiah and four of his very important men to Huldah the prophetess. "Go and ask the Lord about the words found in this book." So the five men left right away.

When they reached Huldah, she was ready with a message from the Lord: "The Lord said He will destroy Jerusalem because the people worship other gods. But tell King Josiah the Lord saw how upset he was. He knows how sorry Josiah is about everything. Therefore the Lord will not destroy Jerusalem in his lifetime."

Josiah was very grateful. He called the Israelites to the temple. Everyone came to hear what King Josiah had to say. When everybody was gathered together, he took out the book with God's laws written in it. When he read the last law they all made a promise to God to do everything that He asked in the Book of the Law.

For the rest of his life Josiah and the whole of Israel served the Lord. What a great story about a little boy who turned a nation back to God!

A Very Special Baby Is Born

And while they were there, the time came for her Baby to be born. She gave birth to her firstborn Son. She wrapped Him snugly in strips of cloth and laid Him in a manger, because there was no lodging available for them.

Luke 2:6-7

Mary was an ordinary girl. She cooked and cleaned and washed the dishes just like all the other girls in Nazareth. She was engaged to Joseph the carpenter. He worked with his saw, hammer and nails the whole day to make things from wood. Mary and Joseph both loved the Lord very much. He had great plans for their lives, but they didn't know about it yet.

One day an angel appeared to Mary. His name was Gabriel. Gabriel greeted Mary and said, "I have good news for you." Mary had a big fright. "Don't be afraid," said Gabriel. "God has a wonderful surprise for you. He has chosen you for a very special task. One of these days you will have a beautiful baby Boy. You must call Him Jesus. He will be great and He will be called the Son of God."

"How will this happen?" Mary wanted to know very worriedly. "I'm not even married yet."

"Don't worry," Gabriel smiled. "The Baby will come from God. God will make Him grow inside you." Gabriel talked to Mary in a comforting voice and she felt a lot better. She just wondered what Joseph was going to say about the Baby. But God took care of it. He also sent an angel to Joseph in a dream. "Get married to Mary," said the angel. "It is God who put the Baby inside her. He wants you to be His father here on earth. You must call Him Jesus. He will deliver people from their sins." When Joseph woke up, he did what the angel told him. He married Mary and looked after her.

The days turned into weeks and later months. Mary's belly grew bigger and rounder. Joseph and Mary couldn't wait to meet their special Baby. There was only one problem. Caesar Augustus wanted to count all the people in his kingdom. They had to list their names in a register. Joseph and Mary had to travel to Bethlehem to be counted there.

When they reached Bethlehem a few days later, they were very tired and hungry. Joseph knocked on all the doors, but no one had a place for them to stay. Finally a friendly innkeeper said, "I can give you a place to sleep in my stable, if you don't mind sleeping there." Mary was very relieved. Joseph made a bed for them to sleep among the cows and the sheep.

That night the Son of God was born. No one in Bethlehem knew that something wonderful was happening. Only Mary, Joseph and the animals in the stable knew. She wrapped the Baby with pieces of cloth and laid Him in a manger so that He could have a cozy and warm place to sleep.

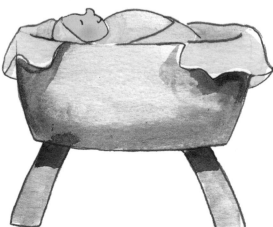

That night in the fields nearby shepherds were looking after their sheep. Suddenly they saw a bright light and an angel of the Lord said, "Don't be afraid! I bring you good news that will bring great joy to all people. Today your Savior has been born in the town of David. He is Christ, the Lord. You will know who He is, because you will find a Baby wrapped snugly in strips of cloth, lying in a manger."

Suddenly there were more angels from heaven ... and more ... and more. Later the sky was filled with angels. They sang: "Glory to God in highest heaven, and peace on earth to those with whom God is pleased." (Luke 2:14)

The shepherds wished the angels would continue singing forever, but they disappeared just as quickly as they came. "Let's go look for the Baby right now!" they said excitedly. It wasn't long before they found Mary and Joseph and the Child lying in the manger. The shepherds couldn't believe it. Everything the angel told them was true. They also told Mary and Joseph about what they had seen and heard.

Mary knew how special Jesus was. She smiled and kept the shepherds' words like precious treasures inside her heart.

In a country east of Bethlehem, there were three wise men. It was their job to look at the stars and to write down everything that they saw. One night a big and bright star appeared. It shined like a giant diamond. The three wise men were very excited. They immediately took out their scrolls. "The star is a sign of the Child who has been born. He will be called King of the Jews," they read.

Quickly they saddled up their camels and filled their bags with gifts for the new King. Then they followed the star to Jerusalem and started asking around about the King who had been born. King Herod heard about it. He was upset. "I am the king, and that is how it will stay!" he told his servants.

Then he thought of an evil plan. He called the three wise men to his palace. "Go and look everywhere for the Child. When you find Him let me know, so that I can also come and worship Him and give Him gifts."

The wise men kept following the star until they found Jesus. They bowed before Him and gave Him gifts of gold, frankincense, and myrrh. That night God warned the wise men in a dream not to return to Herod. The next morning at daybreak they took another road to return to their home.

Mary, Joseph and Jesus were all safe. Jesus grew and grew and was a blessing to Mary and Joseph. One day He would be the Man who would die on the cross to save all people from sin. One day we will meet Jesus in heaven, how exciting that will be!

Jesus Visits the Temple

Three days later they finally discovered Him in the Temple, sitting among the religious teachers, listening to them and asking questions. All who heard Him were amazed at His understanding and His answers.
Luke 2:46-47

Every year Jesus' parents went to Jerusalem for the Passover festival. All the houses and places to sleep were full. The streets were very crowded with people who came from faraway places to the temple.

When Jesus was twelve years old they went up to the feast as usual. When they reached Jerusalem there were so many people that Mary, Joseph and Jesus had to hold on to each other not to get lost in the masses. The people talked, laughed, prayed and sang at the top of their voices. They came to say thank you to God for everything He had done for them during the past year. Jesus watched and listened. He was fascinated by all the wonderful things happening all around Him.

After seven days the feast was over. It was time to go home. Mary and Joseph started the long walk back to their home. By the afternoon, Mary was worried because Jesus had not shown up. "Have you seen Jesus?" she asked friends and family along the way. Everyone just shook their heads.

"I don't think you need to worry," said Joseph. "He will be here soon. You'll see!"

When it started getting dark and everyone began to put up their tents for the night, Jesus was still nowhere to be seen. Now Joseph was also getting worried. He walked up and down looking for Jesus.

"As soon as the sun rises, we'll go back to Jerusalem to look for Him," Joseph promised and wiped a tear from Mary's cheek.

That night Mary and Joseph couldn't sleep. All they were thinking about was that Jesus was missing! Very early the next morning Mary and Joseph got up. They walked as fast as they could back to Jerusalem. They walked up and down the streets looking for Him. After three days they found Him in the temple. He was sitting with the teachers, listening to them and asking them questions. Everyone who heard Him was amazed at His understanding and answers.

All Mary and Joseph could think about was how worried they had been. "Where have You been all this time?" Joseph asked with an angry voice. "We've been looking for You for days!" said Mary.

"Why were you looking for Me? Didn't you know that I must be in My Father's house?" said Jesus.

Mary and Joseph didn't quite understand what Jesus meant. They were just relieved and glad that they had found Him.

Jesus went back to Nazareth with His parents and obeyed them. On their way home Mary thought about everything that had happened. She put her arm around Jesus' shoulder. She couldn't believe He was almost as tall as she was.

But one thing she knew very well: He made her heart and God's heart very happy. All the people He met saw what a special boy He was.

Jesus' Cousin, John the Baptist

But the angel said, "Don't be afraid, Zechariah! God has heard your prayer. Your wife, Elizabeth, will give you a son, and you are to name him John. You will have great joy and gladness, and many will rejoice at his birth, for he will be great in the eyes of the Lord.
Luke 1:13–15

Zechariah was a priest. He and his wife, Elizabeth, wished they could have a child. "I would make him the cutest little clothes," said Elizabeth. "I would tell him stories and carve little figurines from wood for him to play with," said Zechariah. "And at night he could sleep in our bed," smiled Elizabeth. "Oh dear, if only it was true," sighed Zechariah. "We are too old to have children now."

"Don't be sad," Elizabeth told Zechariah. "At least we have each other."

One day Zechariah was busy in the temple. While he burned incense on the altar inside, a great crowd was praying outside. Suddenly an angel appeared at the right side of the altar. "Don't be afraid, Zechariah," the angel said. "God has heard your prayer. Your wife, Elizabeth, will have a baby boy soon. You must name him John. He will bring you joy and gladness, and many people will be happy because of his birth. God has chosen him for a very special task."

Oh, I wish Elizabeth could see the angel! thought Zechariah. "The Holy Spirit will always be with John," the angel continued. "His most important task will be to warn people to stop doing wrong things and to obey the Lord so that they will be ready for His return."

"This all sounds too good to be true," said Zechariah. "How do I know you're telling the truth?" The angel looked at Zechariah with an angry frown, "My name is Gabriel. God sent me. Now, listen! You will not be able to speak until the

day your son is born, because you did not believe what I told you."

Zechariah hurried home. Although he couldn't speak, he couldn't wait to tell the good news to Elizabeth.

Mary, Jesus' mother, was a relative of Elizabeth and was so happy for her. "Just imagine how the two boys will enjoy playing together!" she said.

Finally John was born. Elizabeth and Zechariah's families wanted the boy to be named after his dad. "No, his name must be John," Elizabeth said. "But there isn't anybody in your family with that name?" they complained. "Let's hear what Zechariah has to say."

Zechariah wrote on a piece of paper: "His name is John." Suddenly Zechariah's voice returned. He was so happy that he made up his own song to thank God. The people looked at little John with surprise. They could see that God was with him.

John grew up fast. He loved the desert. He wore clothes from camel skins and ate honey. In the desert

it was always quiet. There he could hear God's voice clearly. He could also talk to God without any distractions.

John started to preach to people by the Jordan River. Many people came to listen to him and gave their lives to God. Then John baptized them in the river. It was a sign of their new life where they didn't want to do wrong things anymore.

Soon people started to call him John the Baptist. He taught the people that he baptized to be honest and to share what they had with others. He also taught them how to make God's heart glad.

"Is this man not perhaps the Lord?" they wondered. John heard what they said. "I baptize you with water, but there is One coming who is greater than I am. He will baptize you with the Holy Spirit. He will light a fire in your hearts that will change your whole lives."

One day Jesus came to the Jordan River. "Will you baptize Me?" asked Jesus. "You don't need to be baptized!" John was surprised. "I want you to baptize Me," said Jesus.

The two cousins walked into the water. A crowd was watching on the banks of the river. Suddenly John saw heaven open up. The Holy Spirit came down like a white dove and flew straight to Jesus. A voice from heaven said, "This is My Son whom I love and I am very pleased with Him." John smiled. He was so grateful that God had chosen him to do this important task of baptizing God's people.

Jairus's Little Girl Comes Back to Life

The crowd laughed at Him because they all knew she had died. Then Jesus took her by the hand and said in a loud voice, "My child, get up!"
Luke 8:53-54

Jairus was a leader of the temple. He hurried to see Jesus. His twelve-year-old daughter was very sick. He knew Jesus could heal her.

After pushing through the crowd to get to Him, Jairus fell down at Jesus' feet. "Please come to my house," he begged. "I know You can heal my little girl. If You can just touch her, I know she will not die. Please!"

"Take Me to your little girl," Jesus said.

Jairus was in a great hurry, but there were so many people that they could hardly move. Among all the people was a woman who had been sick for twelve years. There wasn't any doctor who could heal her. *If I can just touch Jesus' coat, I will be healed,* she thought and pushed forward to reach Jesus.

Suddenly she managed to reach out and touch Him. She couldn't believe it when she immediately felt better.

"Who touched Me?" Jesus wanted to know.

The woman had such a fright that she started shaking. She fell down before Jesus and told Him how she had suffered for so long because of her illness. "That's alright," comforted Jesus, "your days of suffering are over. Now go in peace." While Jesus was busy talking to the woman, Jairus started losing hope. He was so worried about his daughter that he was pacing back and forth.

Just then a messenger came running to them. "Jairus, I have bad news," he said. "Your little girl has died. Jesus doesn't need to come anymore. He can't do anything for her."

Jesus heard everything and said, "Don't be upset. Just believe and your daughter will be well."

When they finally reached Jairus's house, all the people were crying. "Stop crying. She is not dead, only asleep," said Jesus. The people laughed at Jesus because they knew the girl was dead. "You don't know what you're talking about.

We saw with our own eyes that she is dead," they said. But Jesus took her hands and called to her, "My child, stand up!"

Jairus's little girl opened her eyes slowly and looked all around. She saw her mommy and daddy. She saw Jesus smiling. Then she carefully got up and walked around.

"Now you can give her something to eat," said Jesus.

Jairus and his wife were laughing and crying at the same time. "She's alive! Our little girl is alive! Jesus made her alive again!" they said to each other.

Everyone was amazed. The people who had laughed at Jesus couldn't believe their eyes. "Don't tell anyone about what has happened," Jesus said to the parents. They really wanted to do what Jesus had asked, but it was difficult not to tell the whole world about the wonderful thing that had happened!

God still does miracles today. He uses doctors to heal people. Sometimes we become so used to these miracles that we don't see them anymore. Do you know someone who was very sick and is healthy again? Or someone whose heart stopped but the doctors managed to save his or her life? Then you know of a miracle!

A Little Boy Shares His Food

Then Jesus took the loaves, gave thanks to God, and distributed them to the people. Afterward He did the same with the fish. And they all ate as much as they wanted.
John 6:11

Jesus was tired. He was busy teaching the people and healing the sick the whole day. He wanted to be alone for a little while. But everywhere He went, people crowded around Him. When Jesus and His disciples climbed a hill, the people followed.

"Look at all these people," the disciples said to each other. "There are about five thousand men. And then we haven't even counted all the women and children. Where will we buy bread for all these people to eat? It's time they all go home."

"Why don't you make a plan?" Jesus asked.

"Even if we worked for months, we wouldn't have enough money to buy them food," Phillip replied.

"Wait, here is a little boy with a basket!" Andrew spoke up.

"What is in your basket, Son?" one of the disciples wanted to know.

"I have five barley loaves and two fish that my mother packed for me, Sir," the boy answered shyly.

"May we have it?" the disciples asked.

The little boy looked at the disciples. He was so hungry that his tummy was rumbling. Then the boy looked into Jesus' eyes. They were filled with love for him and for the disciples and all the hungry people. Then the boy knew he could trust Jesus with his bread and fish.

"Tell the people to all sit down," Jesus said to His disciples. After everyone found a place on the grassy slopes to sit, Jesus took the bread from the little boy. Then He prayed to God and thanked Him for the food. Then He started giving the food to the people.

The little boy was amazed to see that the fish and bread was not running out! Everybody had more than enough to eat. Even the birds had some crumbs. After everyone finished eating, Jesus said, "Gather the leftover pieces of fish and bread so that nothing is wasted."

The little boy and the disciples walked around among the people and gathered twelve baskets of left-over food. They heard the people talking about Jesus. They said He was God's Messenger who came to earth.

The boy watched as Jesus climbed higher and higher up the hill. He *knew* that Jesus was the King of his heart. *Wait until my family hears what Jesus did with my five pieces of bread and two fish,* he thought.

He turned around and ran home as fast as he could.

God also wants to use us like He did this little boy. We don't need to be rich or big or clever or pretty. We must just be willing to share what we have.

Today at school why not share your sandwich with someone who doesn't have one.

Write Your Own Story

My name is ....

I am .... years old.

I live in ....

My hair color is ....

My skin is ....

My eyes are ....

My favorite food is ....

I like to play ....

My best friend's name is ....

I am special and precious because ....

When I grow up I want to be ....

God loves me very much!